On the Wings of Wonder

The Story of John James Audubon

By Shannen Yauger

Illustrated by Kessler Garrity
Designed by Robin Fight

© 2024 The Good and the Beautiful, LLC
goodandbeautiful.com

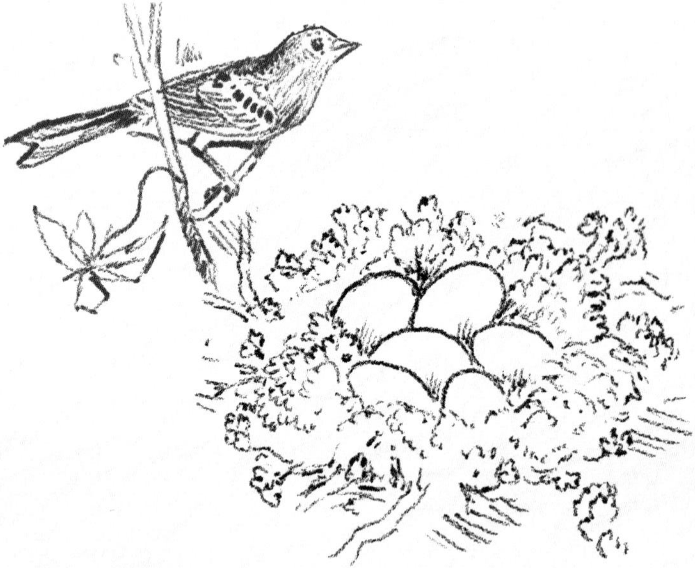

A WILDERNESS ENCOUNTER

In the vast expanse of the Louisiana wilderness, where the ancient trees reached toward the heavens and the joyous sounds of wildlife filled the air, John Audubon found himself immersed in a world of wonder. With a sketchbook in hand and a heart brimming with curiosity, Audubon ventured deep into the landscape. His footsteps were guided by a deep connection to nature and an insatiable desire to understand its secrets.

As he wandered along the moss-covered ground, Audubon's senses came alive. The sweet scent of wildflowers intertwined with the earthy aroma of damp soil. The vibrant hues of birds darting through the foliage caught his eye, and the chorus of their songs filled his ears. Lost in the wilderness, Audubon would often pause to sketch the complex patterns of a fern or the delicate petals of a wildflower. His hand moved with precision, capturing the essence of the natural world on the pages of his sketchbook.

yellow breast

Hooded Warbler (originally mistaken for Selby's Flycatcher)

THE STORY OF JOHN JAMES AUDUBON | 1

On one particular day, as the sun cast golden rays through the canopy above, Audubon stumbled upon a secluded clearing. He gasped in awe as he saw a red-tailed hawk soar gracefully overhead, its wings outstretched, riding the currents of the wind. Heart pounding with excitement, Audubon fumbled for his sketchbook, his hands trembling with anticipation. He knew he had chanced upon a rare and precious moment—a glimpse into the intimate world of a magnificent creature. With careful strokes of his pencil, Audubon sought to immortalize the hawk's majesty. He captured the sweep of its wings, the intensity in its gaze, and the untamed spirit that seemed to emanate from within.

As he worked, a sense of purpose welled up within Audubon. He realized that his art had the power to transport others to these wild places, to let them experience the beauty and awe of the natural world that often remained hidden to those who did not venture beyond the confines of society.

As the red-tailed hawk soared into the distance, Audubon closed his sketchbook, a smile of satisfaction on his face. He knew that this encounter was just the beginning—a prelude to the audacious adventures that awaited him in the unsettled corners of the world.

juvenile in flight

Red-tailed Hawk

2 | ON THE WINGS OF WONDER

John James Audubon was born on April 26, 1785, in the French colony of Saint-Domingue, which is present-day Haiti. He spent his early years surrounded by the lush tropical forests and diverse wildlife of the Caribbean.

His father, a French naval officer, recognized John's fascination with nature and nurtured his curiosity. Together they explored the environment, observing the vibrant birds that filled the trees and the creatures that roamed the land. Their idyllic life was disrupted when political unrest forced the family to flee the island. They embarked on a treacherous journey across the Atlantic, seeking refuge in Nantes, France.

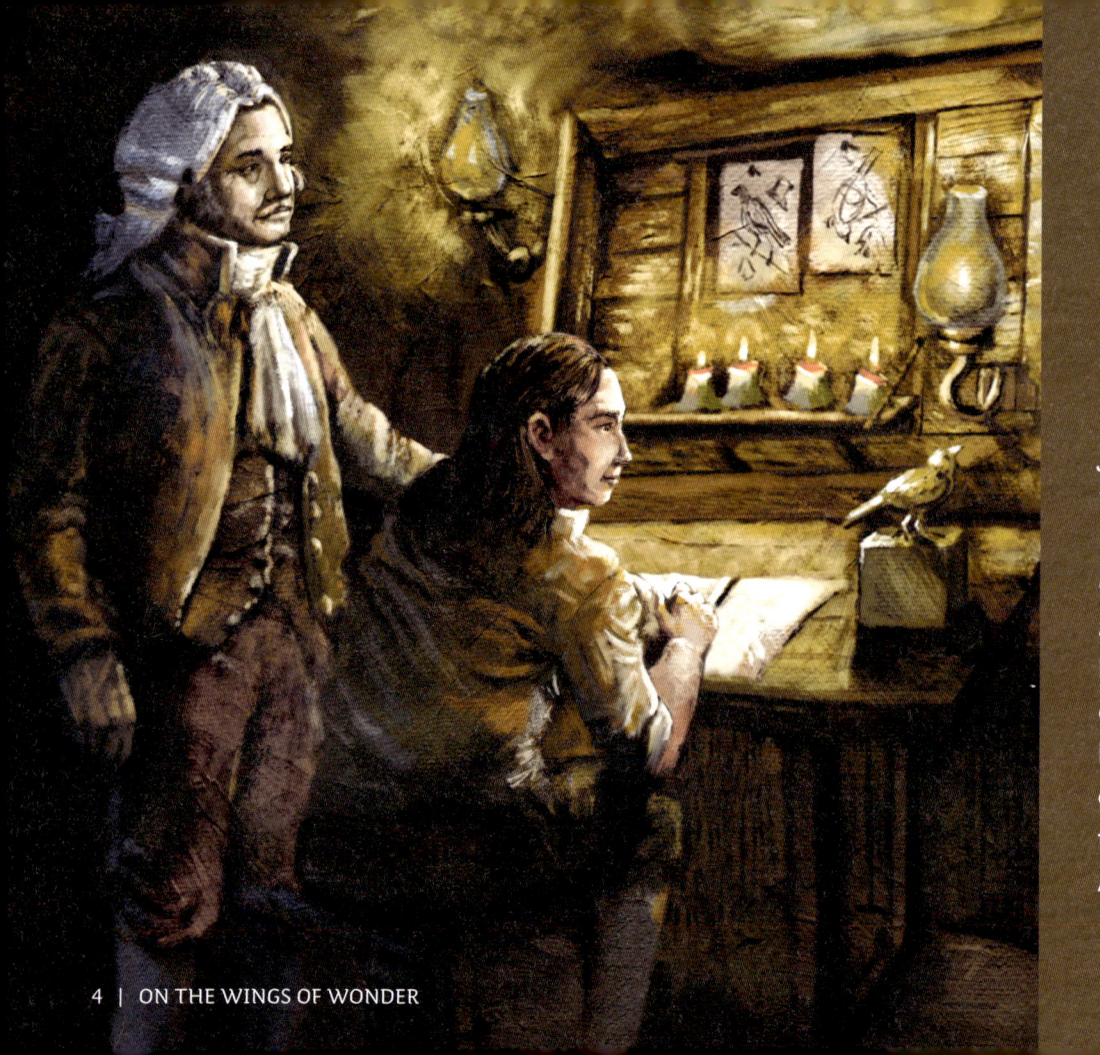

In France, Audubon's passion for art blossomed. He studied drawing and painting, honing his skills and exploring various techniques. However, his true calling lay not just in transferring the world to canvas but also in capturing the essence of its avian inhabitants. Audubon's love for birds and his desire to document their beauty led him to embark on a grand adventure across the vast expanse of the American wilderness.

EXPLORING THE AMERICAN FRONTIER

Audubon arrived in the United States in 1803, a young man filled with dreams and a relentless curiosity. He ventured into the remote lands of the American frontier, armed with his artistic talent, a shotgun, and an insatiable desire to observe and study birds.

Traveling on foot and by boat, Audubon explored the forests, mountains, prairies, and marshlands, tirelessly sketching and documenting the bird species he encountered. His days were filled with long hours of observation, recording the details and habits of birds in his sketchbooks. Audubon's unwavering passion for birds fueled his determination to document every known species in North America. He braved harsh weather conditions, treacherous terrains, and encounters with dangerous wildlife in his pursuit of avian knowledge.

As the seasons shifted and the wilderness transformed, Audubon's insatiable thirst for exploration led him to new horizons. He embarked on a quest to seek out the rare and elusive species that dwelled within the untamed corners of the American landscape.

A MOUNTAINTOP ENCOUNTER

John Audubon stood atop a mountain peak, his gaze spanning a vast expanse of wilderness. The rugged landscape stretched as far as the eye could see, a tapestry of peaks and valleys, forests and rivers. He inhaled deeply, filling his lungs with the crisp mountain air. The solitude of the wilderness soothed him, offering a respite from the clamor of civilization. Audubon felt a deep connection to this pristine landscape—a connection that went beyond words or sketches.

He observed a soaring eagle, its majestic wings outstretched as it rode the thermals high above. Audubon was struck by the bird's graceful movement. He sketched the eagle in flight, capturing its regal presence and the sense of freedom it embodied.

Bald Eagle

larger beak; dense brown feathers on wings

ON THE WINGS OF WONDER

As he descended from the mountain, Audubon encountered a family of grazing deer, their graceful movements echoing the gentle rhythm of the wilderness. He marveled at their delicate features and the quiet strength they possessed. In his sketch, he aimed to convey the serenity they brought to the landscape.

The wilderness spoke to Audubon in ways that words could not express. It reminded him of the interconnectedness of all living things, the delicate balance that sustained ecosystems, and the profound beauty that lay hidden within nature's embrace. With the wilderness calling him forward, Audubon embarked on the next chapter of his remarkable journey. Driven by his love for nature and his unwavering dedication to its conservation, he continued to explore, document, and share the wonders he encountered.

underside of tail is white

White-tailed Deer (also called Common or Virginian Deer)

THE STORY OF JOHN JAMES AUDUBON | 7

With his trusty sketchbook tucked under his arm and a map guiding his way, Audubon set out on a journey that would take him through sprawling forests, meandering rivers, and vast prairies. He sought not only to observe the avian wonders that resided there but also to document their delicate details and capture their essence on paper. His dedication led him to become one of the first people in North America to successfully band a bird for scientific purposes. Audubon tied silver threads around the legs of eastern phoebes, marking the beginning of birdbanding as a method to study migration patterns and behavior.

His travels brought him face-to-face with a multitude of captivating creatures. He witnessed the elegance of great blue herons as they gracefully waded through tranquil marshes, their long necks arched with poise. He marveled at the vibrant plumage of the warblers that flitted among blooming wildflowers like living rainbows.

THE STORY OF JOHN JAMES AUDUBON | 9

Audubon's encounters with nature were not without challenges. He faced untamed wilderness, harsh weather conditions, and occasional setbacks. But his passion burned brightly, fueling his determination to overcome obstacles and push forward in pursuit of his mission.

On one occasion, as Audubon ventured into a dense forest, he found himself entangled in a thicket of brambles. Undeterred, he carefully extricated himself, his determination unyielding. He understood that the path to discovery was not always smooth, but it was through these trials that he grew stronger, both as a naturalist and as an individual.

DEEP IN THE FOREST

John Audubon found himself in the heart of a lush forest, surrounded by towering trees that seemed to touch the sky. The air was thick with the earthy scent of moss and the sweet fragrance of wildflowers. He stood in awe of the majestic beauty that enveloped him. The forest was alive with birdsong, each species contributing its unique voice to the music in the air. Audubon closed his eyes and listened, allowing the enchanting tunes to transport him to another realm.

He spotted a flash of vibrant colors among the branches—a warbler, its feathers adorned with hues of yellow and green. Audubon carefully observed its movements, captivated by its agile flight and melodious song. He sketched the warbler with reverence, capturing its beauty and spirit on paper.

Farther along the forest path, Audubon encountered a family of woodpeckers. Their rhythmic tapping echoed through the trees, a percussion section in nature's grand orchestra. He marveled at their specialized beaks and their ability to find sustenance within the trunks of trees. With each stroke of his pencil, he immortalized their presence in his sketchbook.

diet of beetles and larvae

The forest continued to reveal its secrets—a flock of finches fluttered among the branches, their cheerful chirping adding to the music of the woods. Audubon documented their beautiful patterns, their delicate features, and the sense of joy they brought to the forest with their presence.

Lazuli Bunting (a bunting is a type of finch)

Ivory-billed Woodpecker

Pine Finch

12 | ON THE WINGS OF WONDER

Throughout his journey, Audubon's sketchbook became a treasure trove of vivid illustrations, each stroke of his pencil capturing the essence of the birds he encountered. He poured his heart and soul into his artwork, striving to convey not only their physical attributes but also the spirit that made them truly remarkable.

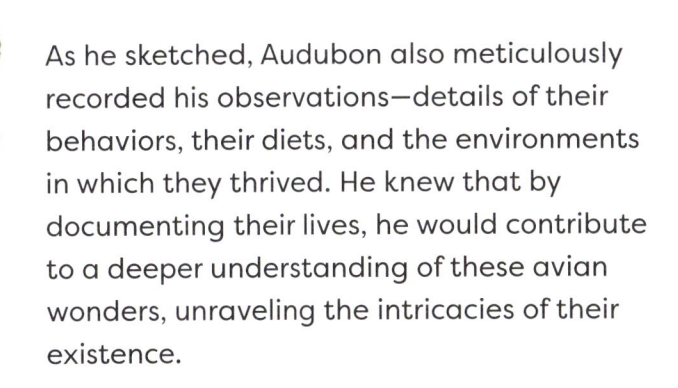

As he sketched, Audubon also meticulously recorded his observations—details of their behaviors, their diets, and the environments in which they thrived. He knew that by documenting their lives, he would contribute to a deeper understanding of these avian wonders, unraveling the intricacies of their existence.

THE ORNITHOLOGICAL EXPEDITION

In the year 1820, John James Audubon embarked on an extraordinary expedition that would shape the course of his career and leave a lasting impact on the field of ornithology. Accompanied by his young assistant, Joseph Mason, Audubon set off on a journey along the Mississippi River, determined to study and document the avian species of North America.

Their expedition began in the bustling city of Cincinnati, Ohio, where Audubon and Mason prepared their supplies, including ammunition, sketching materials, and a large collection of specimen boxes. They secured a flat-bottomed boat, loaded it with provisions, and set sail downstream, their eyes filled with anticipation for the wonders that awaited them.

As they drifted along the mighty Mississippi, Audubon and Mason marveled at the diverse landscapes that unfolded before them.

They encountered dense forests teeming with birdlife,  vast wetlands bustling with waterfowl,  and towering bluffs that offered panoramic views of the river's serpentine path.

THE WETLANDS

John Audubon was immersed in the serenity of a vast wetland. The air was thick with moisture, and the sounds of chirping frogs and buzzing insects filled the atmosphere. Audubon marveled at the unique ecosystem that thrived in this watery landscape.

With his sketchbook in hand, Audubon observed the graceful dance of a heron as it waded through the shallow waters, its long neck poised to strike at unsuspecting prey. He sketched the heron, capturing its elegant form and the tranquility it exuded in this wetland sanctuary.

White Heron

white neck band

Mallard Duck

Moving deeper into the wetlands, Audubon encountered a chorus of waterfowl. Ducks and geese took to the air in flight, their wings beating in harmony. He meticulously captured their diverse plumage and the way they gracefully skimmed across the water's surface.

As Audubon ventured farther into the wetlands, he discovered the hidden world of marsh-dwelling creatures. He observed the intricate web of life, from tiny insects to amphibians and reptiles. With each stroke of his pencil, he depicted the fragile beauty and resilience of these wetland inhabitants.

ON THE WINGS OF WONDER

Audubon and Mason spent their days avidly observing birds in their natural habitats. Audubon's keen eyes and artistic talent allowed him to capture the finest details of each species—their colors, markings, and behaviors. With a rifle at his side, he skillfully collected specimens, which he would later sketch and describe in his notebooks.

18 | ON THE WINGS OF WONDER

Life on the expedition was not without its challenges. Audubon and Mason faced encounters with territorial birds defending their nests, battled swarms of mosquitoes and biting flies, and endured the relentless heat of the summer sun. They navigated treacherous waters, avoiding hidden snags and sandbars that threatened to capsize their boat. However, the hardships were outweighed by the thrill of discovery and the satisfaction of contributing to the knowledge of avian species. Audubon's determination and passion fueled their progress, and Mason's assistance and companionship provided valuable support along the way.

The expedition took them through the heart of the American wilderness, from the vibrant forests of Kentucky and Tennessee to the expansive wetlands of Louisiana. Audubon's sketchbook was filled with breathtaking illustrations of birds, including the iconic American bald eagle, the majestic great blue heron, and the delicate ruby-throated hummingbird.

THE SOUNDS OF THE WILDERNESS

John Audubon ventured deep into the untamed wilderness, his footsteps carrying him farther away from civilization. The dense forest enveloped him, its ancient trees towering overhead, their branches interwoven like a tapestry. As he navigated through the undergrowth, a chorus of sounds filled the air. The rustling of leaves, the melodious trills of birds, and the gentle babbling of a nearby stream created a harmonious chorus that echoed through the woods. His senses heightened, Audubon became attuned to the subtle nuances of the forest. He noticed the interplay of light and shadow, the fragrant scent of wildflowers, and the mesmerizing patterns formed by sunlight filtering through the canopy above.

With each step, Audubon's curiosity grew, fueled by the desire to uncover the secrets of this uncharted territory. He felt a deep connection to the wilderness, a connection that stirred his soul and fueled his passion for exploration.

vibrant patches of red on sides of head

Fox Sparrow

ON THE WINGS OF WONDER

Walking along a narrow path, he stumbled upon a clearing—a natural haven bursting with life. Vibrant wildflowers painted the meadow in a myriad of colors, and butterflies flitted gracefully from one blossom to another. Audubon reached for his sketchbook and pencil, eager to capture the beauty that surrounded him. With precise strokes, he began to translate the scene onto the pages, his hand moving with a sense of purpose.

Carolina Rose

Time seemed to slip away as he immersed himself in his art. He sketched the delicate petals of a wild rose, the graceful curve of a fern, and the patterns adorning the wings of a butterfly. His pencil danced across the page, giving life to the wonders he witnessed. Lost in his creative reverie, Audubon was blissfully unaware of the passing hours.

The sun began its descent, casting long shadows across the meadow. As daylight waned, the forest came alive with nocturnal creatures, their calls blending with the sounds of the night.

Seaside Sparrow
(originally mistaken for a finch)

Audubon's and Mason's encounters with wildlife extended beyond birds. They marveled at the sight of alligators sunning themselves on riverbanks, observed the graceful movements of river otters, and caught glimpses of elusive mammals, such as black bears and white-tailed deer.

Throughout their journey, Audubon and Mason encountered friendly Indigenous people and locals who shared stories and legends about the birds that graced their lands. They learned about the importance of birds in folklore as symbols of freedom, wisdom, and resilience.

As the expedition drew to a close, Audubon and Mason had amassed an enormous collection of specimens and sketches. They returned to settled areas in the eastern United States, where Audubon meticulously transformed his field observations and sketches into lifelike illustrations, showcasing the beauty and diversity of North American bird species. The ornithological expedition propelled Audubon to new heights of acclaim and recognition in the scientific community. His detailed illustrations and groundbreaking observations brought to light previously unknown bird species and provided invaluable insights into their behaviors and habitats.

THE MASTERPIECES UNFOLD

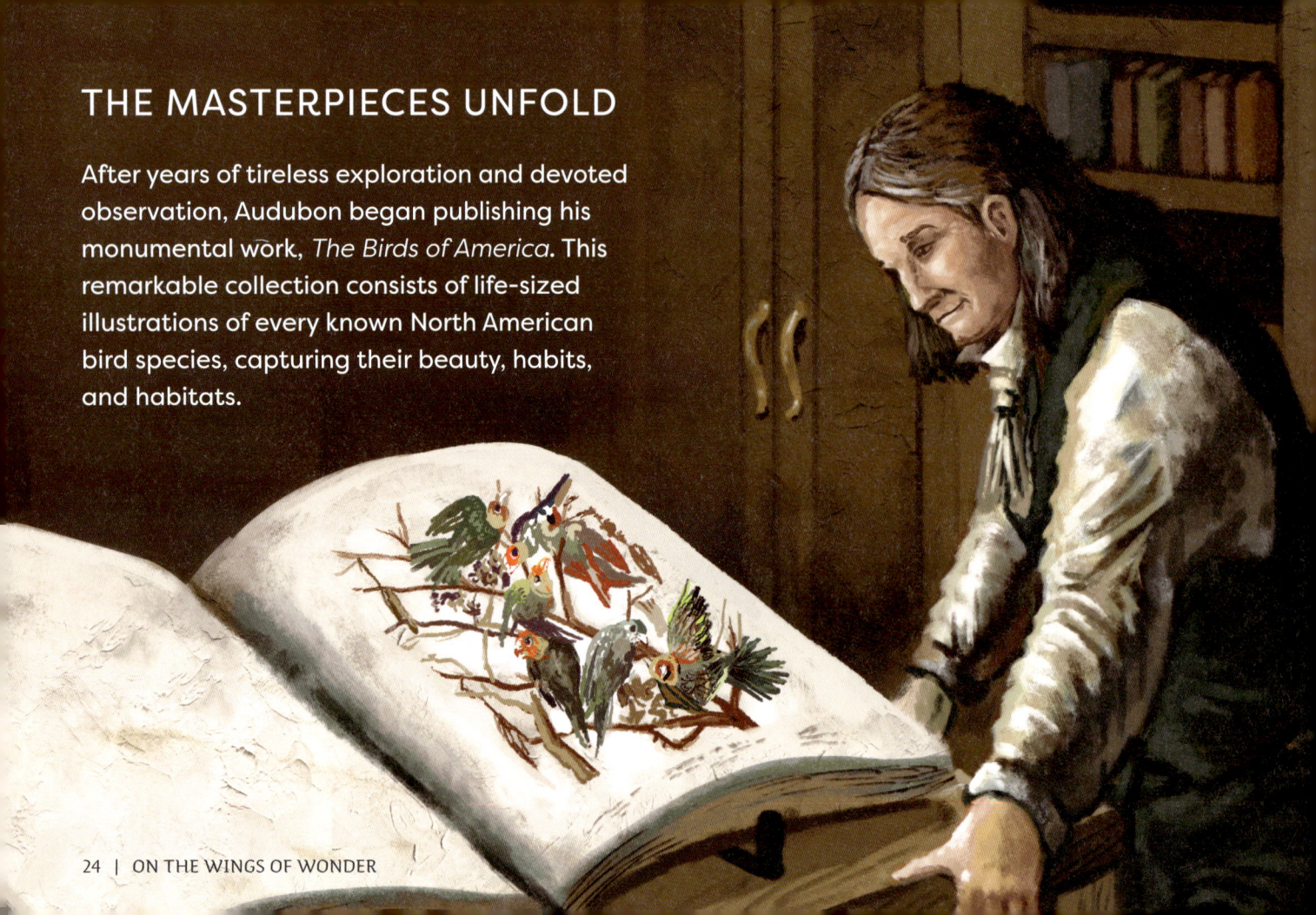

After years of tireless exploration and devoted observation, Audubon began publishing his monumental work, *The Birds of America*. This remarkable collection consists of life-sized illustrations of every known North American bird species, capturing their beauty, habits, and habitats.

IN THE GROVE

In the early light of dawn, John Audubon was nestled in a hidden grove, surrounded by towering trees and a chorus of waking birds. He sat quietly, his sketchbook open on his lap, observing the world awakening around him. The sun's gentle rays filtered through the canopy, casting a golden glow upon the forest floor. Dewdrops clung to blades of grass, glistening like tiny diamonds. Audubon marveled at the beauty of nature, so delicately woven together.

As he traced the colorful petals of a wildflower, a soft breeze whispered through the trees. The enchanting trill of a robin blended with the cheerful chirping of sparrows. With his pencil, he traced the contours of a nearby tree, capturing its strength and resilience. He sketched the patterns of leaves and the veins that carried life-giving sustenance throughout the branches. Each stroke was a tribute to the awe-inspiring scene he witnessed.

feeding young in nest

American Robin

As he completed his sketch, Audubon leaned back against the tree trunk, his gaze fixed on the canopy above. The branches swayed gently in the breeze, casting shifting patterns of light and shade. He marveled at the dance of nature, a choreography unseen by many. In this moment of reflection, Audubon realized that his purpose extended beyond documenting the physical attributes of birds. His mission was to capture the essence of the natural world—the interconnectedness, the delicate balance, and the ever-present beauty that surrounded him. With renewed determination, Audubon closed his sketchbook and rose to his feet. He knew that his journey was far from over. There were still countless wonders to discover, stories to tell, and lessons to learn.

Lincoln's Sparrow

Song Sparrow

26 | ON THE WINGS OF WONDER

He would continue to explore, sketching the birds that graced his path, the landscapes that took his breath away, and the tiny details that made each creature unique. Through his art, he would share the beauty of nature, inspiring others to appreciate and protect the precious wonders that exist beyond the reach of civilization. And so, with the serenade of nature echoing in his heart, Audubon set forth once again, his footsteps carrying him deeper into the wilderness, ready to embrace the next chapter of his extraordinary journey.

American Pipit (originally identified as Prairie Titlark)

The publication of *The Birds of America* brought Audubon international acclaim. The vivid illustrations, meticulously hand-colored, showcased his artistic skill and scientific accuracy. The work became a cornerstone of ornithology and a testament to Audubon's dedication to sharing the world of birds.

A LEGACY OF CONSERVATION

Audubon's contributions extended beyond his artistic and scientific achievements. He recognized the importance of conservation and advocated for the protection of birds and their habitats. As Audubon journeyed through the untamed wilderness, his passion for nature and its preservation grew stronger with each passing day. The vibrant landscapes, the captivating birds, and the delicate balance of ecosystems left an indelible mark on his soul.

In his heart, Audubon carried a profound understanding of the fragility of the natural world. He witnessed firsthand the rapid decline of habitats and the impact human activities can have on nature when not carefully planned. It fueled his determination to bring about change and to inspire others to join him in his mission. With his sketchbook filled with detailed illustrations, Audubon sought to show not only the physical beauty of the birds he encountered but also their spirit, their grace, and their significance within the world.

THE STORY OF JOHN JAMES AUDUBON | 29

In the heart of the wilderness, John Audubon found himself captivated by a mesmerizing scene unfolding before his eyes. He stood on the banks of a shimmering lake, watching as a family of ducks gracefully glided across the water. The ducklings, tiny and vulnerable, followed closely behind their mother, mirroring her every move. Audubon was awestruck by their delicate features and the display of familial unity.

As he sketched the ducks with swift strokes of his pencil, Audubon pondered the interconnectedness of all living things. The ducks relied on the lake for sustenance, their feathers blending seamlessly with the water's surface. The lake, in turn, thrived with abundant life, from fish darting beneath its surface to the insects buzzing around its edges.

Black Jester
(originally identified as American Jester Duck)

female (brown)
male (glossy black)

female

male

Gadwall Duck

30 | ON THE WINGS OF WONDER

As Audubon immersed himself in his artwork, he became acutely aware of the delicate balance that governed the natural world. Each species had its place and purpose. He recalled his encounters with other creatures along his journey—the industrious beavers building their dams, the elegant deer grazing in meadows, and the powerful predators prowling in search of prey. Each had a role to play, a part to fulfill on the earth. He longed for a world where future generations could witness the vibrant plumage of birds, the ancient majesty of forests, and the awe-inspiring diversity of life. It was a vision that propelled him forward, a vision that held the power to inspire change.

American Beaver

As he closed his sketchbook, Audubon vowed to dedicate his life to the preservation of the natural world. He would continue to document its wonders, sharing the stories of its inhabitants and advocating for their protection.

White-tailed Deer

THE STORY OF JOHN JAMES AUDUBON | 31

32 | ON THE WINGS OF WONDER

His artwork resonated with people far and wide, stirring emotions and awakening a sense of wonder. Audubon's illustrations became a bridge between the natural world and society, transcending language and cultural barriers. Through his art, he spoke to the hearts of those who beheld his work.

Audubon's passion and dedication attracted a circle of like-minded individuals—fellow explorers, scientists, and artists who shared his vision. Together they formed a united front, advocating for the conservation and protection of nature's wonders. They organized exhibitions and lectures, showcasing Audubon's illustrations and sharing his message of environmental stewardship. They collaborated with scientists to study and document the ecosystems they encountered, collecting valuable data that would guide conservation efforts.

Audubon's voice grew stronger with each new supporter he gained. His name became synonymous with the preservation of nature, his efforts recognized and respected by both scholars and the general public. He became a beacon of hope, inspiring countless individuals to take action in their own communities.

In the wake of Audubon's legacy, the National Audubon Society was founded in 1905. This organization was created to continue his mission of bird conservation and habitat preservation to this day, engaging millions of people in birdwatching, environmental education, and conservation initiatives. They work tirelessly to protect birds and their habitats, conducting scientific research, advocating for policy changes, and fostering a love for nature in people of all ages.

A LASTING IMPRINT

John James Audubon's legacy endures, reminding us of the power of passion, dedication, and artistry in the pursuit of knowledge and conservation. Through his artistic renderings and scientific contributions, he forever imprinted the beauty of birds on the pages of history. Audubon's impact on the world of ornithology and conservation is immeasurable. His artistic brilliance and his scientific contributions laid the foundation for modern bird study and helped shape our understanding of the natural world.

His story reminds us to appreciate God's creations, to seek understanding, and to be stewards of the fragile ecosystems that sustain life on our planet. Audubon's journey continues to inspire us to explore, to observe, and to protect the delicate balance of nature that surrounds us. The story of John Audubon lives on as a testament to the wonders of the natural world and the indomitable spirit of those who strive to understand and protect it.

Timeline

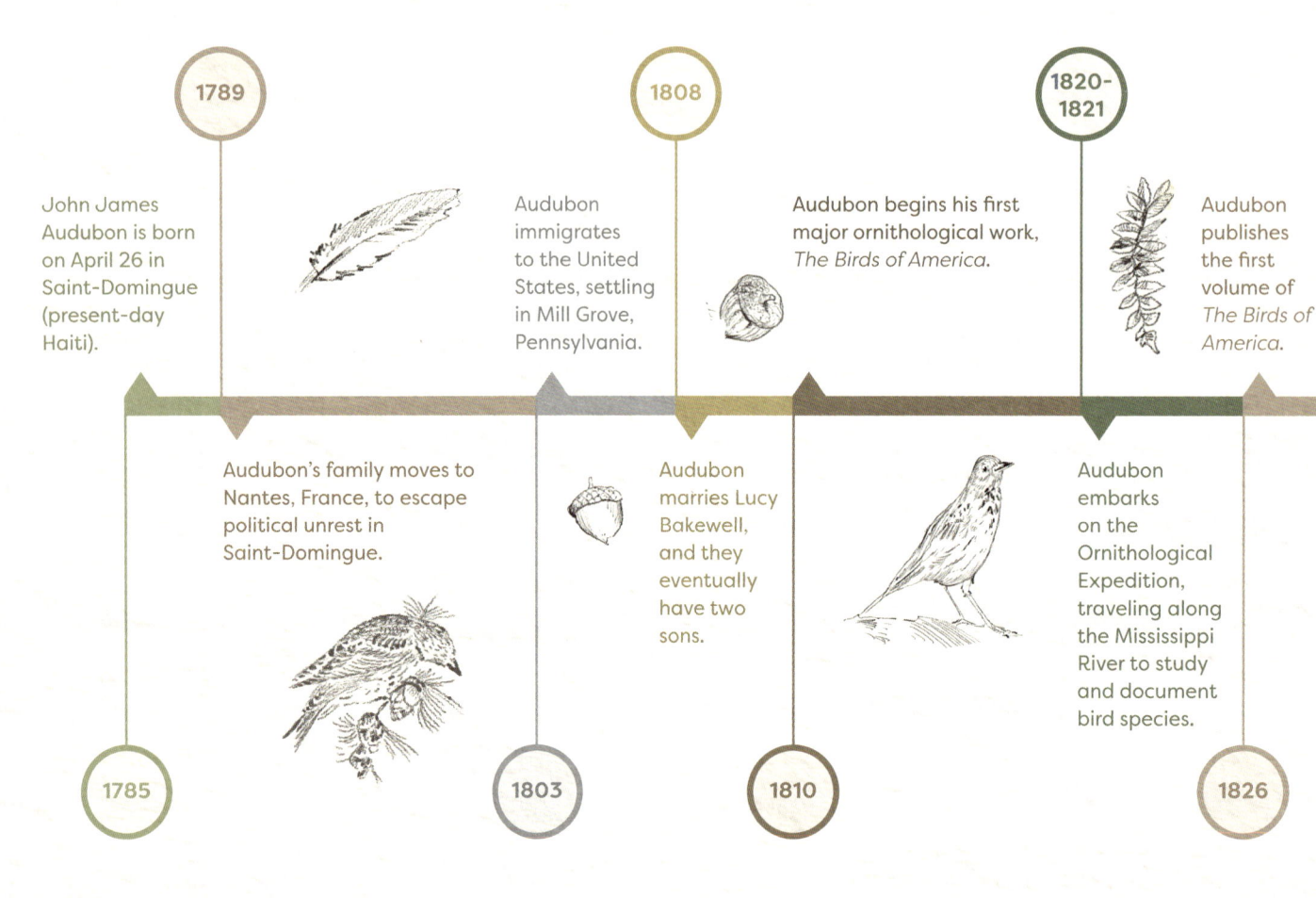

1785 — John James Audubon is born on April 26 in Saint-Domingue (present-day Haiti).

1789 — Audubon's family moves to Nantes, France, to escape political unrest in Saint-Domingue.

1803 — Audubon immigrates to the United States, settling in Mill Grove, Pennsylvania.

1808 — Audubon marries Lucy Bakewell, and they eventually have two sons.

1810 — Audubon begins his first major ornithological work, *The Birds of America*.

1820–1821 — Audubon embarks on the Ornithological Expedition, traveling along the Mississippi River to study and document bird species.

1826 — Audubon publishes the first volume of *The Birds of America*.

1830
Audubon publishes his second major work, *Ornithological Biographies*, providing detailed descriptions and observations of each bird species.

1838
Audubon's health begins to decline, and he spends his remaining years revising and expanding his writings.

1851
The National Audubon Society is founded in his honor, becoming one of the leading organizations dedicated to bird conservation and habitat preservation.

1831
Audubon encounters financial difficulties and travels to Europe to find subscribers and collaborators for his work.

1843
Audubon completes the publication of *The Birds of America* with a total of 435 plates (full-page color illustrations).

1905
John James Audubon passes away on January 27 in New York City at the age of 65.

THE STORY OF JOHN JAMES AUDUBON | 37

Today: Audubon's artistic and scientific contributions continue to inspire bird enthusiasts, artists, and conservationists worldwide. His legacy lives on through the ongoing efforts to protect and appreciate the beauty of birds and their habitats.

38 | ON THE WINGS OF WONDER